TABLE OF CONTENTS

Chapter 15: Optimizing MySQL for the Web: PHP and MySQL Performance Techniques

1. Efficient Database Connections:

2. Fetch Data Optimally:

3. Reduce Query Overhead:

4. Exploit MySQL's Cache with PHP:

5. Leverage PHP Caching Techniques:

6. Avoid N+1 Queries Problem:

7. Optimize Session Handling:

8. Employing Eager Loading:

9. Using Asynchronous Processing:

10. Regularly Update PHP and MySQL:

Chapter 16: Regular Maintenance: Routine Practices for MySQL Health

1. Regularly Check and Optimize Your Database:

2. Perform Regular Backups:

3. Monitor Disk Space:

4. Update Statistics:

5. Check for Errors with `CHECK TABLE`:

6. Archive Old Data:

7. Purge Binary Logs:

8. Monitor Slow Queries:

9. Regularly Review User Privileges:

10. Keep Your MySQL Version Up-to-date:

Chapter 17: Monitoring MySQL: Tools and Tips to Keep Your Database Fit

1. Using MySQL's Built-in Performance Schema:

2. MySQL Workbench:

3. MySQL Enterprise Monitor:

4. Third-Party Tools:

5. Monitoring Slow Queries:

6. Tracking Status Variables:

7. Binary Logs Inspection:

8. Monitor User Activity:

9. Monitor Replication:

10. Setting up Alerts:

Chapter 18: Concurrency Control: Managing Multiple Connections Efficiently

1. Understanding Concurrency:

2. MySQL Concurrency Controls:

3. Transaction Isolation Levels:

4. Optimizing InnoDB for Concurrency:

5. Understanding Locking Granularity:

6. Deadlocks:

7. MySQL's LOCK TABLES and UNLOCK TABLES:

8. Using OPTIMIZE TABLE:

9. Connection Pooling:

10. Using MySQL's max_connections System Variable:

Chapter 19: Performance Tuning: Advanced Techniques to Turbocharge MySQL

1. Understanding the Importance of Performance Tuning:

2. MySQL Performance Tuning Primer Script:

3. Fine-tuning MySQL Server Variables:

4. Using Performance Schema:

5. MySQL Index Optimization:

6. Partitioning:

7. Optimizer Hints:

8. Using EXPLAIN PLAN:

9. MySQL Tuner:

10. Profiling:

Chapter 20: Pushing the Limits: Real-World Case Studies of MySQL Optimization

1. Facebook: Massive Scale MySQL

2. Twitter: Migration to MySQL

3. Booking.com: Database Sharding

4. Wikipedia: Read-Write Splitting and Replication

5. Uber: Schema-less MySQL

CHAPTER 1: STARTING RIGHT: SETTING UP YOUR MYSQL FOR PERFORMANCE

Getting started with MySQL, you want to ensure you're setting things up in a way that supports optimal performance from the get-go. This chapter will guide you through some crucial steps to lay a solid foundation for your MySQL setup.

CHOOSING THE RIGHT MYSQL VERSION

First, you need to select the right MySQL version. As of this writing, the latest stable version is MySQL 8.0. This version brings several enhancements for improved performance, security, and features compared to previous versions.

INSTALLING MYSQL

Once you've decided on the version, it's time to install MySQL. Whether you're using Windows, macOS, or Linux, MySQL offers specific installers for each platform. For instance, here's a command you can use to install MySQL on Ubuntu:

```bash
sudo apt update
sudo apt install mysql-server
```

After running these commands, you'll have MySQL installed and ready for further configuration.

CONFIGURING MYSQL FOR PERFORMANCE

MySQL comes with a default configuration that is designed to be safe and compatible with as many systems as possible, but it may not deliver the best performance for your specific use case. To optimize it, you'll need to adjust certain configuration parameters in the MySQL configuration file, often called "my.cnf" or "my.ini".

One key configuration parameter to adjust is `innodb_buffer_pool_size`. This value should be about 70-80% of your system's total RAM for a dedicated database server:

```bash
[mysqld]
innodb_buffer_pool_size = 4G # (adjust value as needed)
```

Note: Be sure to adjust these values based on the specifics of your system and workload.

CHOOSING THE RIGHT STORAGE ENGINE

MySQL has several storage engines, each suited to different types of workloads. InnoDB is generally a good choice for most applications because it supports transactions and row-level locking. MyISAM can be faster in some cases but lacks these important features.

You can set the default storage engine in your "my.cnf" or "my.ini" file:

bash

[mysqld]

default-storage-engine = InnoDB

CREATING A DATABASE AND TABLES

Once MySQL is configured, it's time to create your database and tables. When creating tables, consider how they'll be used. For instance, if you know you'll be frequently retrieving a certain subset of data, you might want to use that as a basis for your table's primary key.

```sql
CREATE DATABASE my_database;
USE my_database;

CREATE TABLE customers (
    id INT AUTO_INCREMENT PRIMARY KEY,
    name VARCHAR(100),
    email VARCHAR(100),
    signup_date DATE
);
```

In this simple example, we're creating a table for customers with a primary key on the `id` field.

Remember, these initial setups are important, as they can significantly impact the performance of your MySQL server. Starting right will make optimizing easier down the line.

We've only just scratched the surface of setting up MySQL for performance. As we go further in this book, we'll delve deeper into more advanced topics to help you truly unlock MySQL's power and potential.

In the next chapter, we will explore "The Key to Speed: Understanding MySQL Indexing Strategies", where we will dive into the concept of indexing and how it can drastically improve your database's performance. Stay tuned!

CHAPTER 2: THE KEY TO SPEED: UNDERSTANDING MYSQL INDEXING STRATEGIES

Now that you have your MySQL database up and running, it's time to dive into the heart of performance optimization - indexing. Proper indexing is often the difference between a high-performance database and a sluggish one.

THE IMPORTANCE
OF INDEXING

In essence, an index in a MySQL database works similarly to an index in a book. It provides a quick way to look up data without having to scan every row in a table. Indexes are particularly beneficial for read-heavy workloads and large datasets, where scanning the entire table would be inefficient.

CREATING INDEXES

Indexes in MySQL are created using the `CREATE INDEX` command. Consider a table "orders" in your database:

sql

CREATE INDEX idx_customer_id

ON orders (customer_id);

In this example, we're creating an index on the `customer_id` column of the `orders` table. This will speed up any queries that involve searching or sorting by `customer_id`.

CHOOSING THE RIGHT INDEX

Not all indexes are created equal. Depending on your data and query patterns, some indexes will be more effective than others. As a general rule, consider creating indexes on:

1. Columns used in WHERE clauses.

2. Columns used in JOIN conditions.

3. Columns used in ORDER BY clauses.

But remember, while indexes can greatly speed up data retrieval, they can slow down data insertion and updates. This is because each time data is inserted or updated, the index needs to be updated as well.

UNDERSTANDING INDEX TYPES

MySQL supports several types of indexes, each suited to different types of queries:

1. B-Tree Indexes: This is the default index type in MySQL. It's good for general queries and is especially effective for range queries.

2. Hash Indexes: These are used for equality comparisons and are extremely fast. However, they're not useful for range queries.

3. Full-Text Indexes: These are used for full-text search operations.

Here's an example of creating a full-text index on the `product_description` column in a `products` table:

```sql
CREATE FULLTEXT INDEX idx_product_description
ON products (product_description);
```

EXPLORING INDEX CARDINALITY

Index cardinality is the number of unique values in the index. Higher cardinality means more uniqueness, which makes the index more effective. MySQL uses index cardinality to decide the order in which indexes are used.

USING EXPLAIN
TO UNDERSTAND
INDEXING

The `EXPLAIN` statement in MySQL can show you how the MySQL query optimizer uses indexes and can be invaluable for understanding and improving your indexing strategy. For example:

sql

```
EXPLAIN SELECT * FROM orders WHERE customer_id = 100;
```

This will provide a breakdown of how MySQL plans to execute the query, allowing you to see which indexes are being used.

Mastering MySQL indexing is a journey. It involves understanding your data, your query patterns, and the intricacies of MySQL's indexing options. But it's a journey well worth taking. With effective indexing, you can dramatically speed up your MySQL database and create a better experience for your users.

Next up, we'll move on to "Getting the Most of SQL Queries: Optimization Techniques," where we'll look at how to write and structure your SQL queries for optimal performance.

(Note: All commands and configuration settings should be adjusted according to your specific system specifications and requirements. Always remember to back up your data before making significant changes.)

CHAPTER 3: GETTING THE MOST OF SQL QUERIES: OPTIMIZATION TECHNIQUES

Once your MySQL is set up and indexed, the next focus of optimization lies in the SQL queries you run. A well-written query can make the difference between retrieving data instantaneously and leaving a user waiting.

UNDERSTANDING QUERY PERFORMANCE

A query's performance can be affected by several factors, including:

- The structure of the query itself

- The structure and indexing of your database tables

- The volume and distribution of data within your tables

You can use the `EXPLAIN` command to understand the MySQL query optimizer's execution plan and identify potential performance bottlenecks.

OPTIMIZING SELECT STATEMENTS

The `SELECT` statement is one of the most frequently used and therefore one of the most important to optimize. Here are a few strategies:

1. Minimize the amount of data retrieved: Only select the columns you need. Using `SELECT *` is tempting, but it can result in unnecessary data retrieval and slow down your query.

sql

```sql
SELECT first_name, last_name FROM customers;
```

2. Limit the number of rows: Use the `LIMIT` clause to restrict the number of rows returned by your query, particularly when you only need a specific number of records.

sql

```sql
SELECT * FROM orders ORDER BY order_date DESC LIMIT 10;
```

USING WHERE CLAUSE EFFICIENTLY

The `WHERE` clause allows you to filter your SQL queries to retrieve only specific data. Here are some ways to optimize your `WHERE` clause:

1. Use indexes: Indexes can greatly speed up `WHERE` clauses. Make sure you are using indexed columns in your `WHERE` clause whenever possible.

2. Avoid functions: Using functions on columns in your `WHERE` clause can prevent MySQL from using indexes.

```sql
-- Avoid this
SELECT * FROM customers WHERE YEAR(signup_date) = 2023;

-- Do this instead
SELECT * FROM customers WHERE signup_date BETWEEN '2023-01-01' AND '2023-12-31';
```

JOINING TABLES EFFICIENTLY

When you need to combine rows from two or more tables, you use a `JOIN` clause. Improper use of joins can lead to performance issues. Here are some tips:

1. Use explicit join syntax: Instead of using commas to specify multiple tables in the `FROM` clause, use explicit `JOIN` syntax.

sql

-- Avoid this

SELECT * FROM orders, customers WHERE orders.customer_id = customers.id;

-- Do this instead

SELECT * FROM orders JOIN customers ON orders.customer_id = customers.id;

2. Join on indexed columns: Like with `WHERE` clauses, joins on indexed columns are faster.

This chapter gave a glimpse into optimizing SQL queries for MySQL. Keep these techniques in mind as you continue to explore and experiment with your queries. But remember, every database and every query is unique, so always test to ensure your optimizations are having the desired effect.

Up next is "SQL Efficiency: Tips to Write Better SQL Scripts," where we will explore how to write SQL in a way that promotes readability, maintainability, and of course, performance.

(Note: All commands and configuration settings should be adjusted according to your specific system specifications and requirements. Always remember to back up your data before making significant changes.)

CHAPTER 4: SQL EFFICIENCY: TIPS TO WRITE BETTER SQL SCRIPTS

Now that we've looked at some key SQL query optimization techniques, let's turn our attention to the broader topic of SQL efficiency. In this chapter, we will explore tips and best practices for writing better, more efficient SQL scripts.

1. BE SPECIFIC WITH YOUR SELECT STATEMENTS

As previously discussed, avoid using `SELECT *` unless you truly need all columns from the table. Instead, specify exactly what you need to minimize the amount of data retrieved.

sql

```
SELECT first_name, last_name, email FROM customers;
```

2. USE PARAMETERIZED QUERIES

Parameterized queries can increase both security and performance. They allow MySQL to efficiently cache a query and reuse it, minimizing the overhead of parsing SQL statements.

Here's an example in PHP:

```php
$stmt = $pdo->prepare('SELECT * FROM customers WHERE id = :id');
$stmt->execute(['id' => $customerId]);
```

3. USE BATCH INSERTS AND UPDATES

Instead of inserting or updating rows one by one, batch them together in a single SQL statement.

sql

```
INSERT INTO orders (order_id, product_id) VALUES
(1, 101),
(2, 102),
(3, 103);
```

4. OPTIMIZE DATE AND TIME FUNCTIONS

When working with dates and times, it can be tempting to manipulate them with SQL functions. But remember, doing so can often prevent MySQL from using indexes. Always aim to keep your WHERE clause sargable (Search ARGument ABLE).

5. USE UNION ALL INSTEAD OF UNION WHEN POSSIBLE

The `UNION` operator combines the result of two SELECT statements but removes duplicate rows. If you know your SELECT statements do not have duplicates, use `UNION ALL` instead. It's faster because it doesn't need to check for duplicates.

sql

```
SELECT column_name FROM table1
UNION ALL
SELECT column_name FROM table2;
```

6. LIMIT THE SCOPE OF UPDATE AND DELETE OPERATIONS

The `UPDATE` and `DELETE` statements can lock large numbers of rows, impacting database performance. Limit their scope using the `WHERE` clause.

sql

```sql
UPDATE orders SET status = 'Cancelled' WHERE order_id = 101;
```

7. COMMENT YOUR SQL SCRIPTS

Comments aren't just for developers. They can also help DBAs understand the purpose and functionality of a script.

sql

-- This script updates the status of all completed orders

UPDATE orders SET status = 'Completed' WHERE shipped_date IS NOT NULL;

These are just some of the ways to improve your SQL scripts for better performance and readability. Up next, we will dive into "The Art of Troubleshooting: Identifying and Fixing Performance Issues," where we will equip you with the skills to identify and resolve common MySQL performance issues.

(Note: All commands and configuration settings should be adjusted according to your specific system specifications and requirements. Always remember to back up your data before making significant changes.)

CHAPTER 5:
THE ART OF
TROUBLESHOOTING:
IDENTIFYING
AND FIXING
PERFORMANCE
ISSUES

Despite our best efforts to set up MySQL optimally and write efficient SQL scripts, performance issues can arise. The key to resolving these issues is understanding how to identify and troubleshoot them effectively.

1. IDENTIFYING PERFORMANCE ISSUES

The first step in resolving performance issues is to identify them. Here are a few signs that you might be experiencing a MySQL performance problem:

- Slow query execution times

- High CPU usage

- Large amounts of disk I/O

- High network traffic

To diagnose these issues, MySQL provides several tools:

- Slow Query Log: This log contains SQL statements that took more than a specific amount of time to execute. You can enable it by setting the `slow_query_log` variable to 'ON' and `long_query_time` to the number of seconds that define a slow query.

sql
```
SET GLOBAL slow_query_log = 'ON';
SET GLOBAL long_query_time = 2;
```

- Performance Schema: This is a storage engine that collects and provides access to database performance metrics. You can query these metrics just like you would any other MySQL data.

- `SHOW PROCESSLIST` command: This command provides information about the threads currently executing within your MySQL server, which can help you identify any problematic queries or processes.

2. COMMON PERFORMANCE ISSUES AND FIXES

Here are a few common MySQL performance issues and how you can fix them:

- Poorly Written Queries: As we've discussed in previous chapters, inefficient queries can lead to performance issues. Always review your SQL scripts and apply the best practices we've outlined for query optimization and efficient SQL scripting.

- Inadequate Indexing: If your database lacks the necessary indexes, your queries will be slower. Review the chapter "The Key to Speed: Understanding MySQL Indexing Strategies" to ensure you're properly using indexes.

- Table Locking: MySQL uses locking to control simultaneous access to data. However, excessive table locking can slow down your database. To mitigate this, consider using the InnoDB storage engine, which uses row-level locking instead of table-level locking.

- Insufficient Hardware Resources: Sometimes, your hardware may not be sufficient to handle your workload. Consider upgrading your hardware or redistributing your workload across multiple servers.

In the next chapter, "Advanced MySQL: Exploring Less-Known Powerful Features," we will venture beyond the basics to discover advanced MySQL features that can further enhance your database's performance.

(Note: All commands and configuration settings should be adjusted according to your specific system specifications and requirements. Always remember to back up your data before making significant changes.)

CHAPTER 6: ADVANCED MYSQL: EXPLORING LESS-KNOWN POWERFUL FEATURES

So far, we've discussed a range of methods to optimize your MySQL performance. However, MySQL has many advanced features that aren't as widely known, yet can significantly enhance your database's speed and efficiency. In this chapter, we'll take a deep dive into some of these powerful features.

1. MYSQL PARTITIONING

Partitioning is a way of dividing a table into smaller, more manageable pieces, while still allowing you to query it as a single table. Partitioning can significantly improve performance, particularly for large tables. MySQL supports several partitioning types, including RANGE, LIST, HASH, and KEY.

Here is an example of creating a table with RANGE partitioning:

```sql
CREATE TABLE sales (
    sale_id INT,
    sale_date DATE
)
PARTITION BY RANGE( YEAR(sale_date) ) (
    PARTITION p0 VALUES LESS THAN (2022),
    PARTITION p1 VALUES LESS THAN (2023),
    PARTITION p2 VALUES LESS THAN (2024)
);
```

2. FULL-TEXT INDEXES AND SEARCHES

Full-text indexes in MySQL allow you to perform complex word-based searches on text-based data. This can be particularly useful when you need to search through large amounts of text data, such as articles or product descriptions.

Here is an example of creating a full-text index and using it to search:

sql

```
ALTER TABLE articles ADD FULLTEXT (title, body);

SELECT * FROM articles WHERE MATCH(title, body) AGAINST ('+MySQL +Optimization' IN BOOLEAN MODE);
```

3. ONLINE DDL OPERATIONS

Online DDL (Data Definition Language) operations allow you to alter tables while still maintaining availability for DML (Data Manipulation Language) statements. This can significantly minimize downtime when you need to modify a table's structure.

sql

```
ALTER TABLE orders ADD COLUMN order_date DATE, ALGORITHM=INPLACE, LOCK=NONE;
```

4. THE MEMORY STORAGE ENGINE

The MEMORY storage engine creates tables with contents that are stored in memory. Because data retrieval from memory is much faster than from disk, MEMORY tables can be a good choice for temporary or non-critical data.

sql

```sql
CREATE TABLE temp_orders ENGINE=MEMORY AS SELECT * FROM orders;
```

5. MYSQL PSEUDO COLUMN

MySQL supports the use of a pseudo column named `_rowid` for InnoDB tables. The `_rowid` pseudo column acts like an alias for the primary key column or the first unique non-null index of the table. It can be used to speed up some queries.

sql

SELECT _rowid, product_name FROM products WHERE _rowid = 5;

In the next chapter, "Table Design: Best Practices for Performance Optimization," we will discuss how to design your tables for optimal performance in MySQL.

CHAPTER 7: TABLE DESIGN: BEST PRACTICES FOR PERFORMANCE OPTIMIZATION

Table design plays a crucial role in the overall performance of MySQL databases. An optimized table design can significantly reduce the processing time and storage requirements. This chapter will guide you through several best practices to follow when designing your tables for maximum performance.

1. CHOOSE THE APPROPRIATE STORAGE ENGINE

Different storage engines have different strengths and weaknesses. For instance, InnoDB is transaction-safe and has features like row-level locking and foreign key constraints, which are beneficial in many use cases. MyISAM, on the other hand, can be faster for read-intensive workloads but lacks transaction support. Choose the one that suits your needs best.

sql

```sql
CREATE TABLE table_name (

  ...

) ENGINE=InnoDB;
```

2. NORMALIZE YOUR TABLES

Normalization is the process of efficiently organizing data in a database. The main aim is to eliminate redundant data, which could lead to inconsistencies. A well-normalized database is efficient and flexible, leading to better performance.

3. USE PROPER DATA TYPES

Choosing the correct data type for your columns can lead to significant storage and performance improvements. Always use the smallest data type that can correctly store your data.

4. OPTIMIZE COLUMN LENGTHS

In line with the correct data types, ensure that you are also setting optimal lengths for your columns. For example, if a VARCHAR column will never hold more than 100 characters, set its length to 100 rather than the maximum 255.

5. INDEX PROPERLY

We've discussed this in detail in the chapter on indexing strategies. Remember, while indexes can speed up data retrieval, they can also slow down write operations. Carefully consider which columns to index.

6. AVOID NULL WHEN POSSIBLE

NULL columns require additional space and can complicate query writing. If a column will always have a value, set it as NOT NULL.

7. USE FOREIGN KEYS FOR DATA INTEGRITY

Foreign keys ensure the relational integrity of data in associated tables. They also allow for efficient join operations.

sql

```
CREATE TABLE order_items (
  order_id INT,
  product_id INT,
  FOREIGN KEY (product_id) REFERENCES products(product_id)
);
```

8. PARTITION LARGE TABLES

Partitioning can drastically improve performance for large tables. You can partition a table by range, list, hash, or key.

Following these best practices in your table design will lead to significant improvements in the performance of your MySQL database. In the next chapter, "Demystifying Database Engines: InnoDB vs MyISAM," we'll take a closer look at these two popular MySQL storage engines and understand their advantages and trade-offs.

CHAPTER 8: DEMYSTIFYING DATABASE ENGINES: INNODB VS MYISAM

When managing MySQL databases, choosing the right storage engine is a key decision that can greatly affect database performance. MySQL supports a variety of storage engines, but for this discussion, we'll focus on the two most commonly used: InnoDB and MyISAM. Understanding their strengths and weaknesses will enable you to make informed decisions and optimize your database performance.

1. INNODB: TRANSACTION-SAFE AND FEATURE-RICH

InnoDB is a robust, feature-rich engine that supports transactions, foreign keys, and row-level locking.

sql

```
CREATE TABLE example (
  id INT,
  data VARCHAR(100)
) ENGINE=InnoDB;
```

- ACID Transactions: InnoDB is a fully ACID-compliant storage engine, meaning it adheres to the principles of Atomicity, Consistency, Isolation, and Durability. This ensures that your data stays consistent and safe even in cases of system crashes or power losses.

- Row-Level Locking: Unlike MyISAM's table-level locking, InnoDB supports row-level locking, which can greatly improve performance in multi-user environments.

- Foreign Key Constraints: InnoDB supports foreign key

constraints, providing better data integrity and efficient joins between tables.

However, these features come with increased complexity and potential overhead. InnoDB may consume more system resources, such as memory and storage, compared to MyISAM.

2. MYISAM: SIMPLE AND FAST

MyISAM is a simpler and often faster engine, particularly for read-heavy workloads. However, it lacks some of the advanced features of InnoDB.

sql

```sql
CREATE TABLE example (
  id INT,
  data VARCHAR(100)
) ENGINE=MyISAM;
```

- Table-Level Locking: MyISAM uses table-level locking, which is less efficient than row-level locking in multi-user environments. However, for read-heavy or single-user databases, this may not be an issue.

- Less Overhead: MyISAM tables typically require less storage and memory than InnoDB tables, making MyISAM a good choice for smaller systems or for databases where performance is the primary concern.

- No Transaction Support: MyISAM does not support transactions, which can lead to data corruption or loss in the event of a system crash. If data integrity is critical to your application, InnoDB would be a better choice.

Deciding between InnoDB and MyISAM depends largely on your specific use case. For applications that require a high level of data integrity, or for complex applications with many concurrent users, InnoDB is generally a better choice. For simpler applications or read-heavy workloads, MyISAM may offer better performance.

Always remember to thoroughly test your database with realistic data and workloads before settling on a storage engine. In the next chapter, "Mastering Joins: Smart Strategies for Query Optimization," we'll dive into the world of SQL joins and how to use them efficiently in MySQL.

(Note: Always remember to back up your data before making significant changes.)

CHAPTER 9: MASTERING JOINS: SMART STRATEGIES FOR QUERY OPTIMIZATION

SQL joins are indispensable for querying relational databases. They allow us to combine data from multiple tables, creating more complex and informative datasets. However, if not used efficiently, joins can be a major performance bottleneck. This chapter will focus on best practices for optimizing SQL joins in MySQL.

1. UNDERSTAND THE TYPES OF JOINS

MySQL supports several types of joins, including INNER JOIN, LEFT JOIN, RIGHT JOIN, and FULL JOIN. The choice depends on the specific data retrieval need. Understanding these types can help you design queries that yield the right results.

2. USE EXPLICIT JOIN SYNTAX

Using explicit JOIN syntax not only makes your SQL statements easier to read and understand, but also allows MySQL optimizer to better understand your intent and thus generate a more efficient execution plan.

sql

SELECT orders.order_id, customers.customer_name

FROM orders

INNER JOIN customers ON orders.customer_id = customers.customer_id;

3. INDEX JOIN COLUMNS

Creating indexes on the columns involved in the join can dramatically improve performance. Indexes can make lookup operations more efficient and help the database engine find matching rows more quickly.

sql

```sql
CREATE INDEX idx_customer_id ON customers (customer_id);
```

4. AVOID CROSS JOINS WHEN POSSIBLE

CROSS JOINs result in Cartesian products which can lead to huge result sets and performance degradation. Always ensure you specify a condition that links the tables being joined.

5. REDUCE THE NUMBER OF ROWS BEFORE JOINING

Perform operations to reduce the number of rows before a join. This could include filtering rows using a WHERE clause, or aggregating data using GROUP BY.

sql

```sql
SELECT orders.order_id, AVG(orders.amount), customers.customer_name
FROM orders
INNER JOIN customers ON orders.customer_id = customers.customer_id
WHERE orders.order_date BETWEEN '2023-01-01' AND '2023-12-31'
GROUP BY orders.order_id;
```

6. BE CAREFUL WITH NULLS IN JOINS

Remember, joining on columns that can contain NULL values can produce unexpected results, as NULLs are not considered equal to each other in SQL.

Joining tables effectively and efficiently is a cornerstone of database optimization. Implementing these strategies can help you boost your MySQL performance and ensure your queries run smoothly.

In the following chapter, "Stored Procedures: Leveraging MySQL's Built-in Functionality for Speed," we'll delve into the world of stored procedures and how they can contribute to a faster, more efficient MySQL database.

CHAPTER 10: STORED PROCEDURES: LEVERAGING MYSQL'S BUILT-IN FUNCTIONALITY FOR SPEED

In this chapter, we will examine how we can leverage stored procedures to optimize the performance of MySQL. Stored procedures are routines that are stored in the database and can be repeatedly called. This allows us to encapsulate complex operations, reduce network traffic, and provide improved performance.

1. INTRODUCTION TO STORED PROCEDURES

A stored procedure is a set of SQL statements stored in the database itself, assigned a name, and executed as a unit. They can take parameters, perform operations, and optionally return results.

Here's an example of a simple stored procedure that retrieves all the orders from a specific customer:

```sql
DELIMITER //
CREATE PROCEDURE GetOrders(IN customer_id INT)
BEGIN
  SELECT * FROM orders WHERE orders.customer_id = customer_id;
END //
DELIMITER ;
```

You can then call this stored procedure like so:

```sql
CALL GetOrders(101);
```

2. USE STORED PROCEDURES FOR COMPLEX LOGIC

Stored procedures can contain complex logic and calculations that might be cumbersome or inefficient to perform in the application layer. By encapsulating this logic into a stored procedure, we can keep the logic in one place and reuse it.

3. STORED PROCEDURES ENHANCE PERFORMANCE

Stored procedures are precompiled and stored in the database. This leads to faster execution as the database engine saves a parsing and compiling step for the SQL statements in the stored procedure.

4. REDUCED NETWORK OVERHEAD

With stored procedures, you can execute a batch of SQL code on the server side, eliminating the need to send multiple lengthy SQL statements over the network.

5. SECURITY BENEFITS

Stored procedures can provide a layer of security between the user interface and the database. They can restrict direct access to the database by only exposing certain stored procedures to users.

6. ERROR HANDLING

MySQL provides error handling capabilities in stored procedures using DECLARE, SIGNAL and RESIGNAL statements. This can help prevent unexpected behaviors from propagating to the user.

As powerful as stored procedures are, they should be used judiciously. They can add complexity to your database schema, and debugging can be more difficult than in regular SQL queries or in your application code.

In the next chapter, "Caching in on Performance: Effective MySQL Caching Techniques", we'll discuss how caching can be used as an effective technique to speed up MySQL performance. Stay tuned!

CHAPTER 11: CACHING IN ON PERFORMANCE: EFFECTIVE MYSQL CACHING TECHNIQUES

In this chapter, we'll explore how effective MySQL caching techniques can dramatically enhance performance by reducing the load on your database and speeding up data retrieval.

1. THE PRINCIPLE OF CACHING

Caching is the process of storing copies of frequently accessed data in a place where it can be accessed more quickly. For MySQL, this often means storing the results of queries or even entire tables in memory.

2. MYSQL QUERY CACHE

MySQL's query cache stores the text of a SELECT statement together with the corresponding result sent to the client. If an identical statement is received, the server can then retrieve the results from the cache rather than executing the statement again.

To enable it, you can adjust the 'query_cache_size' system variable:

sql

```
SET GLOBAL query_cache_size = 1048576;
```

However, as of MySQL 8.0, the query cache is deprecated due to scalability issues. Therefore, it's recommended to rely on other caching techniques or third-party solutions for newer MySQL versions.

3. INNODB
BUFFER POOL

For InnoDB tables, MySQL provides the InnoDB buffer pool. This cache holds frequently accessed data blocks in memory. The larger the buffer pool, the more InnoDB acts like an in-memory database, reading data from disk once and then accessing the data from memory during subsequent reads.

You can adjust its size using the 'innodb_buffer_pool_size' system variable:

sql

```sql
SET GLOBAL innodb_buffer_pool_size = 268435456;
```

4. THIRD-PARTY CACHING SOLUTIONS

For more advanced caching requirements, you might want to consider third-party solutions like Memcached or Redis. These can be used to store the results of complex queries, session data, or other temporary data that your application uses frequently.

5. PROPER CACHING STRATEGIES

Caching isn't just about enabling it and forgetting it. A proper caching strategy involves understanding your workload and tuning your cache configuration to match. Too much caching can use up system resources, while too little might not give you the performance boost you need.

6. MONITORING CACHE PERFORMANCE

Tools like the Performance Schema can help you monitor how effectively your cache is working and help identify areas for improvement.

Remember, caching is a powerful tool for enhancing the performance of MySQL databases, but it is not a silver bullet. Always consider it as part of a broader performance optimization strategy.

In the next chapter, "Exploring MySQL Configuration: Tweaking for Performance", we will delve into various MySQL configuration settings that can help optimize your database's performance.

CHAPTER 12: EXPLORING MYSQL CONFIGURATION: TWEAKING FOR PERFORMANCE

In this chapter, we'll delve into the world of MySQL configuration settings, understanding their impact on performance, and learning how to tweak them to our advantage.

1. THE IMPORTANCE OF MYSQL CONFIGURATION

The default MySQL configuration isn't designed for high-performance systems. The default settings ensure MySQL's stability and compatibility but may not fully exploit the available resources. Understanding and adjusting these settings can significantly improve database performance.

2. CONFIGURING INNODB BUFFER POOL

We've touched on this in the previous chapter, but it's worth repeating: the InnoDB buffer pool is a crucial performance feature. It caches data and indexes in memory to reduce disk I/O operations. The 'innodb_buffer_pool_size' configuration setting should ideally be set to about 70-80% of system memory for a dedicated database server.

3. ADJUSTING KEY BUFFER SIZE

For MyISAM tables, 'key_buffer_size' is the equivalent of InnoDB's buffer pool. It determines the amount of memory used for indexing. A larger value will result in faster index-related operations but at the expense of system memory.

4. CONFIGURING MYSQL QUERY CACHE

As discussed in the previous chapter, MySQL's query cache can provide a substantial performance boost by caching the result set of SELECT queries. You can adjust its size using 'query_cache_size'. Be aware though, this feature is deprecated in MySQL 8.0 and above.

5. TEMP TABLE CONFIGURATION

Temporary tables are a vital part of complex SELECT statements. The 'max_heap_table_size' and 'tmp_table_size' variables limit the memory a temporary table can use before it's converted to an on-disk table, which is significantly slower.

6. THREAD HANDLING

MySQL creates a separate thread for each client connection. The number of simultaneous connections is controlled by the 'max_connections' setting. If too high, it may consume excessive system resources. If too low, it could prevent necessary connections.

7. LOGGING

Logging operations can slow down MySQL. If the 'general_log' or 'slow_query_log' are enabled, make sure to monitor the disk space usage.

8. USING MYSQL TUNER SCRIPT

MySQL Tuner is a Perl script that analyzes your database server and provides configuration recommendations based on the server's stats and workload. It's a great tool for finding a good starting point for manual tuning.

9. CONSTANT MONITORING AND TUNING

Tweaking MySQL's configuration is not a one-time operation. Continual monitoring and adjustments are necessary to maintain an optimal performance level. Tools like Performance Schema, Slow Query Log, and MySQL Workbench can help.

In the next chapter, "Understanding the Query Execution Plan for Better Performance", we will examine how to understand and optimize the MySQL query execution plan for better performance.

CHAPTER 13: UNDERSTANDING THE QUERY EXECUTION PLAN FOR BETTER PERFORMANCE

Understanding the Query Execution Plan (QEP) is crucial for improving performance in MySQL. The QEP gives a glimpse into how the MySQL server interprets your SQL queries and decides on the best approach to retrieve or update data.

1. WHAT IS A QUERY EXECUTION PLAN?

The Query Execution Plan is MySQL's blueprint for executing a SQL query. MySQL's query optimizer generates this plan, taking into account several factors like indexes, table structure, and the database configuration.

2. UNDERSTANDING MYSQL EXPLAIN

To access the QEP, we use the EXPLAIN command in MySQL. This command provides information on how MySQL executes a query.

For example, if we had a query like `SELECT * FROM customers WHERE customer_id = 100;`, we would use EXPLAIN as such:

sql
EXPLAIN SELECT * FROM customers WHERE customer_id = 100;

This will return a table with various columns explaining how MySQL intends to execute the query. Let's look at some key columns:

- select_type: This can be SIMPLE (a simple SELECT query without any subqueries or UNION), SUBQUERY, or UNION.

- table: Shows which table this part of the plan is dealing with.

- type: Describes the join type. Types include ALL (full table scan), index (full index scan), range (an index scan over a given range), among others.

- possible_keys: Indicates which indexes MySQL can choose from.

- key: The key (or index) that MySQL decided to use.

- rows: The estimated number of rows to be examined.

- Extra: Contains additional information about how MySQL will execute the query.

3. INTERPRETING THE QUERY EXECUTION PLAN

Reading and understanding the QEP allows us to identify potential performance issues in our query. If we see that MySQL is doing a full table scan (type: ALL) for a query that should be able to use an index, we might need to rethink our indexes or the structure of the query.

4. MAKING ADJUSTMENTS BASED ON QEP

Based on the insights from the QEP, we can make necessary adjustments to our queries or database structure for better performance. This might involve adding or changing indexes, adjusting the structure of a query, or modifying our database schema.

5. LIMITATIONS OF EXPLAIN

While EXPLAIN is powerful, it has limitations. It only provides an estimate based on the statistics available to the optimizer, and the actual performance might differ. It also does not provide information on subqueries in the FROM clause.

Understanding the Query Execution Plan is an essential skill for anyone looking to optimize MySQL performance. By utilizing this information, we can get insight into how our queries are executed and how we might improve them. In the next chapters, we will look at other advanced MySQL features and techniques to further optimize performance.

CHAPTER 14: HANDLING LARGE DATASETS: TECHNIQUES FOR EFFICIENT DATA MANAGEMENT

In this chapter, we delve into the strategies and techniques for handling large datasets in MySQL efficiently. We'll look at strategies for loading, querying, and maintaining large volumes of data, while minimizing the performance impact.

1. IMPORTANCE OF EFFICIENT DATA MANAGEMENT

When your database starts dealing with large datasets (gigabytes to terabytes and beyond), efficiency and optimization become crucial. Without proper management, large datasets can degrade performance and slow down query execution.

2. DATA LOADING TECHNIQUES

Loading large volumes of data efficiently is essential. MySQL's LOAD DATA INFILE command can quickly load data from CSVs and other delimited file formats. Disabling indexes, foreign key checks, and unique checks during data loading can also drastically improve the loading speed.

3. PARTITIONING

Partitioning allows MySQL to treat parts of a table as independent units, providing several benefits for large tables. It can help query performance, simplify maintenance operations, and provide a form of data archiving.

4. INDEXING LARGE DATASETS

Indexing strategy is even more critical with large datasets. Covering indexes can provide significant performance benefits. However, remember that large indexes also require more storage and maintenance.

5. DATA ARCHIVING

Data archiving is a good practice when dealing with vast amounts of historical data. Archiving old data can lead to a more responsive and manageable system. MySQL does not directly support automatic data archiving, but strategies can be implemented at the application level.

6. USING FEDERATED TABLES

Federated storage engine allows access to data stored on a remote MySQL database. This engine can be a good choice when dealing with large datasets that span multiple databases.

7. EFFECTIVE QUERYING

Efficient querying becomes even more important with large datasets. Techniques such as avoiding select *, limiting the result set, and effective use of JOINs can significantly improve performance.

8. REGULAR MAINTENANCE

Large datasets require regular maintenance to ensure continued performance. This includes routine tasks such as updating statistics for the optimizer, defragmenting tables, and checking for errors.

9. USING NOSQL FEATURES

MySQL 5.6 and above come with NoSQL support, which can improve the performance when working with large datasets. NoSQL can be faster for certain types of data access, especially when dealing with large, unstructured data.

In the next chapter, "Optimizing MySQL for the Web: PHP and MySQL Performance Techniques", we will explore how to optimize MySQL in the context of a web application, focusing on the interaction between PHP and MySQL.

10. MANAGING SERVER RESETS: OVERWRITING DEFAULT VALUES

In a typical MySQL setup, certain configuration values may get overwritten when the server resets. This is due to the way MySQL uses configuration files. When MySQL starts up, it reads the configuration settings from several files in a specific order, with later files overwriting the settings in earlier ones.

For example, MySQL first reads the settings in the 'my.cnf' file located in the base installation directory. Then, it reads from '/etc/my.cnf', and so forth. Therefore, if the same variable is set in multiple files, the last read would be the effective value.

In a hosting environment like Plesk, the system takes control of MySQL's configuration settings to ensure optimal operation based on its understanding of the environment's needs. However, you might want to overwrite some of these settings based on your application's specific requirements.

In the case of Plesk, you can change the MySQL configuration by editing the 'my.cnf' file, which is typically located at '/etc/my.cnf'. However, note that Plesk often resets this file to its default values, particularly during updates.

To avoid your settings being overwritten, Plesk provides a way to persist custom configuration changes:

1. Create a custom configuration file. It is recommended to name this file 'custom.cnf' and place it in the '/etc/mysql.d/' directory.

2. Add your custom settings in this file.

3. Restart the MySQL server for the changes to take effect.

Plesk automatically includes all '.cnf' files from the '/etc/mysql.d/' directory when the MySQL server starts. Therefore, settings in your 'custom.cnf' file will overwrite the default settings, and they will persist even if Plesk resets the 'my.cnf' file.

CHAPTER 15: OPTIMIZING MYSQL FOR THE WEB: PHP AND MYSQL PERFORMANCE TECHNIQUES

Working with MySQL and PHP in a web environment requires a keen understanding of how these two technologies interact and how to leverage their strengths for optimal performance. This chapter covers strategies and techniques to optimize MySQL performance specifically in the context of PHP applications.

1. EFFICIENT DATABASE CONNECTIONS:

PHP scripts usually open a new connection to the MySQL server for each web page request. A more efficient method is to use persistent connections via `mysqli_pconnect` or `PDO::ATTR_PERSISTENT`. However, use these judiciously as they can lead to server resource issues if not managed properly.

2. FETCH DATA OPTIMALLY:

Minimize data transfer between MySQL and PHP by fetching only the data you need. Use precise SQL queries, limit returned data with the `LIMIT` clause, and avoid using `SELECT *` unnecessarily.

3. REDUCE QUERY OVERHEAD:

Use prepared statements or parameterized queries to reduce parsing overhead for similar queries. They also provide built-in protection against SQL injection attacks.

4. EXPLOIT MYSQL'S CACHE WITH PHP:

MySQL's query cache can significantly speed up PHP applications by storing the result set of a query. When an identical query is encountered, the result is fetched from cache instead of executing the query again.

5. LEVERAGE PHP CACHING TECHNIQUES:

Apart from MySQL's caching mechanisms, PHP provides several caching tools like APC, XCache, and OpCache. These tools cache PHP opcode, thereby reducing the time spent in parsing and compiling PHP scripts.

6. AVOID N+1 QUERIES PROBLEM:

This is a common problem where an application executes one query to fetch a list of items, and then for each item, executes another query to fetch related data. This can be resolved by using joins or subqueries.

7. OPTIMIZE SESSION HANDLING:

PHP's default session handling stores session data in files which may not scale well. Consider using session handling databases like Memcached or Redis for better performance and scalability.

8. EMPLOYING EAGER LOADING:

In object-relational mapping (ORM), data required by an object is not loaded until it's actually accessed. This can lead to performance issues. Eager loading solves this by loading all necessary data upfront.

9. USING ASYNCHRONOUS PROCESSING:

For long-running PHP scripts, consider asynchronous processing. Tasks are run in the background, allowing the application to continue processing other tasks.

10. REGULARLY UPDATE PHP AND MYSQL:

Ensure that PHP and MySQL are regularly updated to leverage performance improvements and new features that come with each release.

Optimizing PHP and MySQL performance is a continuous process of monitoring, identifying bottlenecks, and applying best practices and strategies. Always measure before and after implementing optimizations to ensure they have the desired effect.

CHAPTER 16: REGULAR MAINTENANCE: ROUTINE PRACTICES FOR MYSQL HEALTH

Consistent maintenance is critical for ensuring the long-term performance and stability of your MySQL database. In this chapter, we'll cover some routine practices that you can adopt to maintain the health of your MySQL database.

1. REGULARLY CHECK AND OPTIMIZE YOUR DATABASE:

Running the `OPTIMIZE TABLE` command can help reclaim unused space and defragment the data file. However, remember that it locks the tables during the operation.

sql

OPTIMIZE TABLE employees, departments;

2. PERFORM REGULAR BACKUPS:

Establishing a regular backup schedule is crucial. The `mysqldump` utility can be used for this purpose.

shell

```
mysqldump -u username -p database_name > backup.sql
```

3. MONITOR DISK SPACE:

Databases grow over time, and running out of disk space can bring your application to a halt. Monitor your disk space usage and plan for capacity expansion if needed.

4. UPDATE STATISTICS:

MySQL uses internal statistics for query optimization. Run `ANALYZE TABLE` to update these statistics periodically.

sql

```sql
ANALYZE TABLE employees, departments;
```

5. CHECK FOR ERRORS WITH `CHECK TABLE`:

The `CHECK TABLE` command can be used to verify the integrity of your tables and should be run periodically to catch any potential issues.

sql

CHECK TABLE employees, departments;

6. ARCHIVE OLD DATA:

If your database handles time-series or historical data, consider implementing an archiving strategy to move older data to slower, cheaper storage.

7. PURGE BINARY LOGS:

Binary logs are used for replication and recovery. However, they can take up a significant amount of space. Make sure to purge them periodically using the `PURGE BINARY LOGS` command.

sql

```sql
PURGE BINARY LOGS BEFORE '2023-04-22 22:46:26';
```

8. MONITOR SLOW QUERIES:

Enable the slow query log to catch and optimize inefficient queries. Here's how you can enable it:

sql
```
SET GLOBAL slow_query_log = 'ON';
```

9. REGULARLY REVIEW USER PRIVILEGES:

As a security measure, periodically review and revoke any unnecessary privileges granted to the database users.

10. KEEP YOUR MYSQL VERSION UP-TO-DATE:

Regularly update your MySQL version to benefit from the latest security patches, bug fixes, and performance improvements.

Maintenance is an ongoing task that helps in preventing many performance and security issues. Set up a schedule for these tasks and monitor your database's health and performance regularly for an efficient and secure database environment.

CHAPTER 17: MONITORING MYSQL: TOOLS AND TIPS TO KEEP YOUR DATABASE FIT

To maintain an optimized MySQL environment, constant monitoring is essential. This chapter explores various tools and techniques for effective MySQL monitoring.

1. USING MYSQL'S BUILT-IN PERFORMANCE SCHEMA:

The Performance Schema is a storage engine that helps troubleshoot performance issues and resource usage. It collects and stores statistics about server events like waits, stages, and statements.

sql
```
SELECT                        *                        FROM
performance_schema.events_statements_summary_by_digest;
```

2. MYSQL WORKBENCH:

MySQL Workbench provides server status visibility and performance dashboard tools to monitor MySQL instances, showing details about system resources, server status variables, and more.

3. MYSQL ENTERPRISE MONITOR:

For users with an Oracle subscription, MySQL Enterprise Monitor offers real-time visibility into the performance and availability of all your MySQL databases.

4. THIRD-PARTY TOOLS:

Several third-party tools can provide detailed insights, such as Percona Monitoring and Management (PMM), SolarWinds Database Performance Analyzer, and Nagios.

5. MONITORING SLOW QUERIES:

As discussed in previous chapters, the MySQL slow query log can be a valuable resource. Regularly check this log to spot and address performance-draining queries.

6. TRACKING STATUS VARIABLES:

MySQL's SHOW STATUS command provides server status information, helping identify potential issues.

sql

SHOW STATUS LIKE 'Threads_connected';

7. BINARY LOGS INSPECTION:

Binary logs, critical for replication and recovery, can grow large over time. Regular monitoring can ensure they don't consume too much disk space.

8. MONITOR USER ACTIVITY:

Monitoring user activity can help track inefficient queries, and maintain security by identifying suspicious activities.

sql

```
SHOW PROCESSLIST;
```

9. MONITOR REPLICATION:

For databases using replication, it's essential to keep an eye on the health of your slave servers.

sql

SHOW SLAVE STATUS\G;

10. SETTING UP ALERTS:

Most monitoring tools provide functionality to set up alerts for certain conditions (like reaching storage limit). Alerts can help preemptively address potential issues before they affect performance.

By using these tools and techniques, you can keep your database in good health, spot potential issues before they become serious problems, and keep your MySQL database running efficiently.

CHAPTER 18: CONCURRENCY CONTROL: MANAGING MULTIPLE CONNECTIONS EFFICIENTLY

When dealing with a database, it's common to encounter multiple users or processes trying to access data simultaneously. This is where concurrency control comes into play. This chapter will discuss how to manage multiple connections effectively in MySQL.

1. UNDERSTANDING CONCURRENCY:

Concurrency refers to the ability of a database to handle multiple operations simultaneously. However, this can lead to conflicts, making concurrency control critical to maintaining data integrity and performance.

2. MYSQL CONCURRENCY CONTROLS:

MySQL implements two types of locks to manage concurrency: shared locks and exclusive locks. Shared locks allow multiple transactions to read (select) a resource simultaneously, but not change it. Exclusive locks allow only one transaction to either read or write a resource.

3. TRANSACTION ISOLATION LEVELS:

Isolation levels determine how locks are applied and how transactions impact each other. MySQL supports four transaction isolation levels: READ UNCOMMITTED, READ COMMITTED, REPEATABLE READ (default), and SERIALIZABLE.

sql

```sql
SET TRANSACTION ISOLATION LEVEL READ COMMITTED;
```

4. OPTIMIZING INNODB FOR CONCURRENCY:

The InnoDB storage engine is built to handle a high level of concurrency, and its performance can be optimized by adjusting certain variables such as `innodb_thread_concurrency`, `innodb_concurrency_tickets`, `innodb_commit_concurrency`, and `innodb_read_io_threads`.

5. UNDERSTANDING LOCKING GRANULARITY:

Locking granularity determines the size of the data portion locked by a single lock action. InnoDB supports row-level locking, which offers better performance but at a cost of higher system overhead.

6. DEADLOCKS:

A deadlock happens when two or more transactions permanently block each other by each holding a lock on a resource the other needs. InnoDB automatically detects and resolves deadlocks by rolling back one of the transactions.

7. MYSQL'S LOCK TABLES AND UNLOCK TABLES:

MySQL allows you to manually lock and unlock tables. This is usually done when performing operations that cannot be done within a single transaction.

sql

LOCK TABLES table_name READ;

8. USING OPTIMIZE TABLE:

OPTIMIZE TABLE can be used to reclaim the unused space and to defragment the data file.

sql

OPTIMIZE TABLE table_name;

9. CONNECTION POOLING:

Connection pooling allows you to manage connections for reuse, reducing the overhead of creating and closing connections for each client's requests. MySQL Connector/J has built-in support for connection pooling.

10. USING MYSQL'S MAX_CONNECTIONS SYSTEM VARIABLE:

The `max_connections` system variable defines the maximum permitted number of simultaneous client connections. By default, it's set to 151. Be careful while adjusting this variable, as too high a number can lead to the server running out of memory.

sql
```
SET GLOBAL max_connections = 200;
```

Managing multiple connections efficiently is a complex task, but with a solid understanding of the underlying principles of concurrency and by using the right tools and techniques, it can be successfully achieved.

CHAPTER 19: PERFORMANCE TUNING: ADVANCED TECHNIQUES TO TURBOCHARGE MYSQL

In this chapter, we explore advanced techniques for performance tuning in MySQL. Performance tuning involves enhancing database speed and efficiency through a variety of strategies and tools.

1. UNDERSTANDING THE IMPORTANCE OF PERFORMANCE TUNING:

Performance tuning helps ensure your database runs efficiently, minimizes latency, optimizes resource usage, and provides a smooth and fast user experience.

2. MYSQL PERFORMANCE TUNING PRIMER SCRIPT:

This open-source tool provides an excellent starting point for MySQL performance tuning. It provides suggestions for adjustments to MySQL server variables to enhance performance.

3. FINE-TUNING MYSQL SERVER VARIABLES:

Server variables like `innodb_buffer_pool_size`, `query_cache_size`, `tmp_table_size` and `max_heap_table_size` can have a significant impact on performance.

sql

```
SET GLOBAL innodb_buffer_pool_size=268435456;
```

4. USING PERFORMANCE SCHEMA:

The Performance Schema is a storage engine that collects and provides detailed performance metrics. Understanding its usage helps in identifying bottlenecks and tuning SQL queries.

5. MYSQL INDEX OPTIMIZATION:

Indexing is crucial for good performance, but over-indexing can lead to slower write operations. The key is to ensure that the most frequently used columns in WHERE and JOIN conditions are indexed.

6. PARTITIONING:

Partitioning allows you to distribute portions of individual tables across a file system based on rules, helping to improve performance and management of large tables.

7. OPTIMIZER HINTS:

MySQL supports a flexible hinting syntax that allows you to control the query optimizer. It enables influencing the optimizer's decision-making process without changing the semantics of the query.

sql
```
SELECT /*+ NO_RANGE_OPTIMIZATION(t1) */ * FROM t1
WHERE key1 = 1;
```

8. USING EXPLAIN PLAN:

The EXPLAIN statement in MySQL provides information about how MySQL executes a query. Understanding how to read the output is crucial to identify potential bottlenecks.

sql
EXPLAIN SELECT * FROM table_name WHERE key1=1;

9. MYSQL TUNER:

MySQL Tuner is a Perl script that analyzes your MySQL performance and, based on the statistics it gathers, gives recommendations which variables you should adjust to increase performance.

10. PROFILING:

MySQL provides a built-in profiling tool that can help you measure the resource consumption by different stages of query execution, thereby helping in identifying bottlenecks and tuning performance.

sql

```sql
SET profiling = 1;
```

Performance tuning is both an art and a science, and it requires a solid understanding of database principles and a keen attention to detail. With these advanced techniques, you'll be well on your way to having a well-optimized, high-performance MySQL database.

CHAPTER 20: PUSHING THE LIMITS: REAL-WORLD CASE STUDIES OF MYSQL OPTIMIZATION

In this chapter, we take a deep dive into several real-world case studies of MySQL optimization. Understanding how other organizations have navigated their database performance challenges will provide practical insights and strategies to tackle your own.

1. FACEBOOK: MASSIVE SCALE MYSQL

Facebook, one of the largest users of MySQL, has pushed the boundaries of the database's scalability. They employ a range of techniques, including partitioning, custom-built tools for global data consistency, and extensive performance monitoring. Facebook's engineers optimized InnoDB, a MySQL storage engine, for compression, resulting in significant space and I/O operations savings.

2. TWITTER: MIGRATION TO MYSQL

Twitter migrated their Tweet storage from a Ruby on Rails object store to MySQL. They chose MySQL due to its maturity, performance, cost-effectiveness, and widespread knowledge within their engineering team. A key part of this transition was developing their data access library to provide transactional consistency and to handle sharding.

3. BOOKING.COM: DATABASE SHARDING

Booking.com, a world-leading travel platform, implemented database sharding to handle high loads on their databases. They use SpockProxy, a MySQL proxy that supports database sharding. Each shard runs on a separate server, increasing overall system performance and allowing for high availability.

4. WIKIPEDIA: READ-WRITE SPLITTING AND REPLICATION

Wikipedia runs on MariaDB, a MySQL fork, and uses replication for load balancing and backup. They implemented a read-write splitting mechanism where read requests are load-balanced across several replicas, and write requests go to a primary server. This technique allowed them to handle a massive volume of read requests without overloading the primary server.

5. UBER: SCHEMA-LESS MYSQL

Uber, in their pursuit of high availability and geographic locality, moved away from Postgres to a schemaless MySQL model. In their 'schemaless' design, MySQL was primarily used as a highly available, distributed key-value store. They built a trigger system on top of MySQL, named Schemaless Triggers, to handle replication across data centers.

Learning from these real-world case studies allows us to understand the practical applications of the techniques and strategies discussed in this book. It's a testament to the flexibility and power of MySQL and how it can be used to optimize performance at scale.

[1]: "Under the Hood: Building and open-sourcing RocksDB". Facebook Engineering. November 2013. <https://engineering.fb.com/2013/11/18/core-data/under-the-hood-building-and-open-sourcing-rocksdb/>

[2]: "New Tweets per second record, and how!". Twitter Engineering Blog. August 2013. <https://blog.twitter.com/engineering/en_us/a/2013/new-tweets-per-second-record-and-how.html>

[3]: "MySQL sharding at Booking.com". Booking.com Developers. February 2019. <https://developers.booking.com/blog/mysql-sharding-at-booking.com>

[4]: "Wikipedia's MySQL infrastructure". Wikimedia Foundation. November 2020. <https://wikitech.wikimedia.org/wiki/MariaDB>

[5]: "The Uber Engineering Tech Stack, Part II: The Edge and Beyond". Uber Engineering Blog. March 2017. <https://eng.uber.com/tech-stack-part-two/>

www.ingramcontent.com/pod-product-compliance
Lightning Source LLC
La Vergne TN
LVHW051338050326
832903LV00031B/3608